Predators in the Wild

Great White Sharks

by Kathleen W. Deady

Scientific Consultant:
Jody Byrum
Science Writer
SeaWorld, San Diego

CAPSTONE
HIGH-INTEREST
BOOKS

an imprint of Capstone Press
Mankato, Minnesota

Capstone High-Interest Books are published by Capstone Press
151 Good Counsel Drive, P.O. Box 669, Mankato, Minnesota 56002
http://www.capstone-press.com

Library of Congress Cataloging-in-Publication Data
Deady, Kathleen W.
    Great white sharks/by Kathleen W. Deady.
    p. cm.—(Predators in the wild)
    Includes bibliographical references (p. 31) and index.
    ISBN 0-7368-0786-1
    1. White shark—Juvenile literature. [1. White shark. 2. Sharks.] I. Title.
II. Series.
QL638.95.L3 D43 2001
597.3'3—dc21   00-009987

Summary: Describes great white sharks, their habits, where they live, their
hunting methods, and how they exist in the world of people.

Editorial Credits

Blake Hoena, editor; Karen Risch, product planning editor; Timothy Halldin,
    cover designer and illustrator; Katy Kudela, photo researcher

Photo Credits

awfoto.com, cover
Carl Roessler/Bruce Coleman Inc., 15
James D. Watt/Mo Yung Productions/www.norbertwu.com, 6, 9, 10 (top),
    10 (middle), 10 (bottom), 27
Jeff Rotman, 8, 22, 24
Innerspace Visions/Tom Campbell, 11, 12; Ron & Valerie Taylor, 14, 16; Richard
    Hermann, 17 (top right); James D. Watt, 17 (bottom right), Doc White,
    21; Marty Snyderman, 28
Norbert Wu/www.norbertwu.com, 18
TOM STACK & ASSOCIATES/Randy Morse, 17 (top left); Therisa Stack,
    17 (bottom left); David B. Fleetham, 20

1 2 3 4 5 6 06 05 04 03 02 01

Table of Contents

Common names: Great white shark; also known as maneater, white pointer, white death, blue pointer, Tommy shark, and uptail.

Scientific name: *Carcharodon carcharias*

Average length: Great white sharks grow 14 to 18 feet (4.3 to 5.5 meters) long.

Average weight: Great white sharks weigh between 1,500 and 4,000 pounds (680 and 1,800 kilograms).

Coloring: Great white sharks are dark gray, blue, or olive-brown on top and white on the bottom.

Life span: Scientists estimate great white sharks live between 30 and 100 years.

Scales: Great white sharks are covered with tiny, overlapping scales called dermal denticles. These scales are smooth when rubbed forward and rough when rubbed backward.

Habitat: Great white sharks live in water over continental shelves. They also live near island coasts, reefs, and shoals.

Prey: Great white sharks eat fish, other sharks, sea lions, seals, dolphins, whales, and sea turtles.

Behavior: Great white sharks are solitary animals. They live and hunt alone. Great white sharks are the only sharks that poke their heads above water. They do this to view their surroundings.

In This Chapter:

* Great white sharks mostly live in shallow water.
* Great white sharks have streamlined bodies.
* Great white sharks are a type of fish.

Chapter 1

Great White Sharks

Great white sharks hunt many kinds of prey. They may eat fish, sea lions, and seals.

Size

Great white sharks are the largest predatory shark. Great white sharks average 14 to 18 feet (4.3 to 5.5 meters) in length. They weigh between 1,500 and 4,000 pounds (680 and 1,800 kilograms).

Male and female great white sharks grow at different rates. Males become adults in about nine years. Female great white sharks usually grow larger than males. They become adults in about 13 to 15 years.

Great white sharks often swim in shallow water.

Species

Great white sharks are fish. Like all fish, they are aquatic vertebrates. They live in water and have a backbone.

Scientists divide fish into groups called classes. Sharks are in the Chondrichthyes class. Animals in this class have skeletons made out of cartilage.

This strong tissue is flexible and lightweight.

Scientists divide sharks further into families. Great white sharks are in the Lamnidae family. This group includes fast-swimming sharks such as mako and salmon sharks.

Pups

Female great white sharks do not lay eggs. Instead, their young are born alive and ready to hunt. Their young immediately swim away on their own after birth.

Young sharks are called pups. Scientists do not know much about great white pups. They believe female great white sharks give birth to between two and ten pups in a litter.

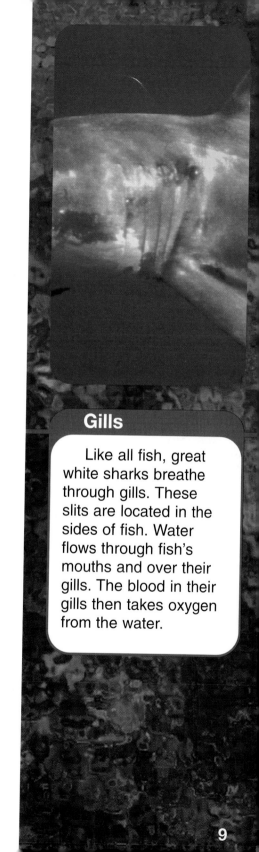

Gills

Like all fish, great white sharks breathe through gills. These slits are located in the sides of fish. Water flows through fish's mouths and over their gills. The blood in their gills then takes oxygen from the water.

Dorsal fin

Pectoral fin

Caudal fin

Swimming

Great white sharks have streamlined bodies. Their bodies are tapered at both ends. This rounded shape allows water to flow smoothly over and around their bodies.

Great white sharks' fins help them swim. Their dorsal fins are on their back. Great white sharks use their dorsal fins for balance. Pectoral fins are on their sides. Great white sharks use these fins to move up and down in the water. The caudal fin is on their tail. Great white sharks sway this fin back and forth to move forward. They also use their caudal fin to move side to side.

Great whites do not have bones. Their skeletons are made of cartilage. This tissue allows great white sharks to bend and twist their bodies as

Great white sharks can bend their bodies as they swim.

they chase prey. It also allows them to turn quickly as they swim.

Habitat

Great white sharks live in temperate waters. These waters usually are between 53 and 75 degrees Fahrenheit (12 and 24 degrees Celsius).

Great white sharks live in waters over continental shelves. These shallow, flat areas are parts of continents. They spread out from the shore and are covered by water.

Great white sharks usually are found in shallow water. They most often stay in water less than 330 feet (100 meters) deep. They may even swim in water as shallow as 3 feet (1 meter). But great white sharks can swim as deep as 4,200 feet (1,280 meters).

In This Chapter:

* Great white sharks are carnivores.

* Great white sharks can smell blood in water.

* Great white sharks have powerful jaws.

The Hunt

Great white sharks are carnivores. They eat
meat. Their diet includes fish such as tuna,
salmon, and halibut. Great white sharks also
eat sea mammals such as dolphins, seals, and
sea lions. They sometimes eat sea birds, otters,
and sea turtles.

Great white sharks seek prey in coastal
waters. They swim near shores, reefs, or shoals.
Many types of prey live in these shallow
water areas.

Great white sharks sometimes eat carrion.
They find these dead animals at sea. They may
even eat food waste from ships.

Great white sharks can smell blood in water.

Senses

Great white sharks rely on their senses to hunt. They have excellent hearing. Scientists believe great white sharks can hear noises in the water up to 825 feet (250 meters) away.

Sharks have a strong sense of smell. They can detect small amounts of blood at great

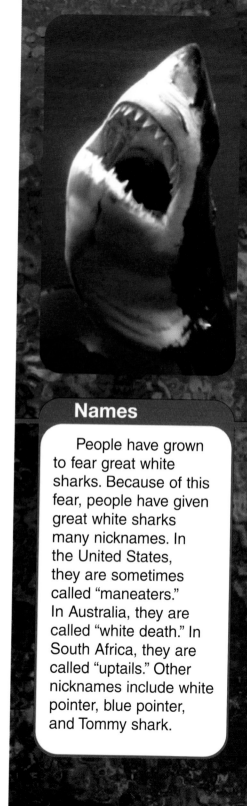

distances. The smell of blood attracts great white sharks.

Great white sharks feel vibrations in the water with their lateralis system. This system consists of a row of sensory pores that runs from head to tail. Inside these small openings are hair-like nerve endings. The nerve endings help great white sharks feel movement in the water.

Animals give off small electrical impulses. Great white sharks can sense the electrical impulses from other animals. They have cells in their jaws and snouts called "ampullae of Lorenzini." These cells detect electricity. Great white sharks can detect the location of their prey with these cells.

Names

People have grown to fear great white sharks. Because of this fear, people have given great white sharks many nicknames. In the United States, they are sometimes called "maneaters." In Australia, they are called "white death." In South Africa, they are called "uptails." Other nicknames include white pointer, blue pointer, and Tommy shark.

Teeth

Great white sharks' teeth grow in rows. Teeth in the back rows move forward to replace old or lost teeth. Great white sharks may use nearly 30,000 teeth in their lifetime.

Jaws and Teeth

Great white sharks have powerful jaws. Strong muscles clamp their jaws shut with tons of pressure as they bite.

Great white sharks' jaws are not hinged like people's jaws. Instead, their upper and lower jaws move separately. This allows great white sharks to open their jaws wide. Great white sharks can swallow large amounts of food at a time.

Great white sharks have long, sharp teeth. Their teeth can be up to 3 inches (7.6 centimeters) long. Great white sharks' teeth are shaped like triangles. The edges of their teeth are serrated. These notches help their teeth cut through prey's flesh.

What Great Whites Eat

Sea Lions

Fish

Seals

Dolphins

In This Chapter:

* Great white sharks attack by surprise.

* Great white sharks' coloring hides them.

* Great white sharks strike quickly.

The Kill

Great white sharks attack by surprise. They locate their prey. They then swim quickly toward it from below and behind. Great white sharks can swim 10 to 15 miles (16 to 24 kilometers) per hour when attacking prey.

Great white sharks' coloring helps them stay hidden from their prey. Their backs are dark gray, blue, or olive-brown. From above, these colors look similar to the ocean floor. Great white sharks' undersides are off-white. From below, this coloring looks like the water above.

Great white sharks open their mouths wide as they attack.

The Strike

Great white sharks do not see their prey as they attack. They roll their eyes into their sockets.

This action protects their eyes as they strike their prey.

Great white sharks raise their snout as they are about to strike. They also drop their lower jaw and move their upper jaw forward. This jaw positioning allows great white sharks to take large bites out of their prey. They move their lower jaw forward and up to bite.

Great white sharks then clamp their jaws shut on their prey. They shake and spin their bodies as they attack. This movement tears large pieces of flesh away.

Great white sharks do not chew their food. They swallow it whole or in large chunks.

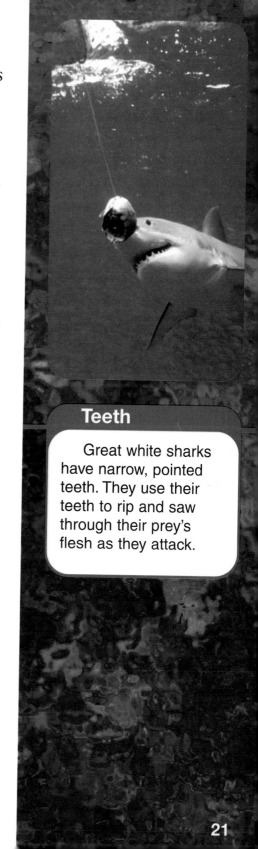

Teeth

Great white sharks have narrow, pointed teeth. They use their teeth to rip and saw through their prey's flesh as they attack.

Great white sharks swallow their food in large chunks.

Weakening Their Prey

Great white sharks try to weaken their prey. They may strike prey quickly and then swim away. Great white shark bites can be large. These wounds may cause their prey to lose great amounts of blood and become weak.

Myth: Great white sharks are bloodthirsty killers. They like to eat people.

Fact: Great whites do not prey on people. Scientists believe that sharks may mistake people for prey. Sharks may think a swimmer is an injured animal. Great white sharks usually stop their attack when they discover the mistake.

Myth: Great white sharks kill large numbers of people.

Fact: In the last 10 years, less than 100 people have been attacked by great white sharks. This number is small compared to other animals such as dogs and poisonous snakes.

In This Chapter:

* Great white sharks rarely attack people.

* Some people hunt sharks for food.

* Great white sharks live in many places.

Chapter 4

n the World of People

For centuries, people have feared great white sharks. Many people believe that they often attack swimmers and surfers at beaches. People also believe that great white sharks may attack divers or people shipwrecked at sea.

Great white sharks have attacked people. But these attacks are very rare. In the 1990s, less than 100 people were attacked by great white sharks. Of these attacks, only 10 people died. Great white sharks attack people by mistake. They may think these people are an injured animal such as a fish or a seal.

Yellow represents the great white shark's range.

Range

Great white sharks live in coastal waters.
They most often are found near the coasts of
North America, Australia, and South Africa.
Great white sharks also live along the coasts of
Japan and South America.

Great white sharks also can be found
swimming in other areas. Many great white
sharks live in the Mediterranean Sea. This sea is
between Europe and Africa.

Threats to Sharks

Great white sharks have no natural predators.
No animals in the wild hunt great white sharks.

But people are a threat to great white sharks. People hunt them for many reasons.

People use great white sharks' body parts for many things. Soap, perfume, and skin cream can be made out of the oil from sharks' livers. People grind shark skeletons into fertilizer. This material nourishes plants. People also may eat shark meat.

Some people hunt great white sharks for fun and sport. They compete to catch the biggest shark.

Fishers often accidentally kill great white sharks and other sharks. The sharks get caught in their fishing nets. Sharks also may get caught in nets people place around beaches. These nets protect swimmers from sharks.

Protection

People protect themselves from sharks in many ways. They put up nets in the water around beaches. They set up electrical barriers. These devices create electrical pulses that sharks sense and will not swim through. Scientists and divers who study sharks use sharkproof cages. People also have invented special suits that protect divers from shark bites.

Scientists do not know how many great white sharks exist.

Scientists' Concerns

Scientists are concerned about the future of great white sharks. They do not know how many great white sharks exist in the world. It is difficult to track their numbers accurately. Great white sharks live in many places. But scientists believe that fewer great white sharks exist in the wild today than in the past.

Great white sharks produce few young. Scientists worry that people are killing great white sharks faster than they can reproduce. Great white sharks may one day become extinct. They then will have died out.

People are working to prevent the extinction of great white sharks. The governments of South Africa, Australia, and the United States have passed laws to protect great white sharks. They prevent people from placing nets that may harm great white sharks. They also prevent fishers from selling their body parts. These efforts may help prevent great white sharks from becoming extinct.

aquatic (uh-KWAT-ik)—living or growing in water

carnivore (KAR-nuh-vor)—an animal that eats meat

carrion (KAIR-ee-uhn)—dead animal flesh

cartilage (KAR-tuh-lij)—a strong, elastic tissue that connects bones in most animals; sharks' skeletons are made out of cartilage.

continental shelf (KON-tuh-nehn-tuhl SHELF)—a shallow, sloping area of the sea floor near a coastline

extinct (ek-STINGKT)—to have died out

streamlined (STREEM-lined)—designed to move easily and quickly through air or water

vertebrate (VUR-tuh-brit)—an animal that has a backbone

To Learn More

Cerullo, Mary M. *The Truth About Great White Sharks.* San Francisco: Chronicle Books, 2000.

Dietz, Heather. *The Great White Shark.* The Underwater World of Sharks. New York: Rosen, 2001.

Martin, James. *Great White Sharks: the Ocean's Most Deadly Killers.* Animals & the Environment. Mankato, Minn.: Capstone Books, 1995.

Maynard, Christopher. *Sharks.* Informania. Cambridge, Mass.: Candlewick Press, 1997.

Useful Addresses

Busch Gardens Tampa Bay
P.O. Box 9158
Tampa, FL 33674

SeaWorld San Diego
500 SeaWorld Drive
San Diego, CA 92109-7904

Mote Marine Laboratory
1600 Ken Thompson
    Parkway
Sarasota, FL 34236

Vancouver Aquarium
P.O. Box 3232
Vancouver, BC V6B 3X8

Internet Sites

All About Sharks
http://www.EnchantedLearning.com/subjects/
sharks

SeaWorld/Busch Gardens Animal Bytes
http://www.seaworld.org/animal_bytes/
greatwhiteab.html

Shark School
http://www.sdnhm.org/kids/sharks/index.html

Index